FISH

BY SUE BRADFORD EDWARDS

Essential Library

An Imprint of Abdo Publishing
abdobooks.com

ABDOBOOKS.COM

Published by Abdo Publishing, a division of ABDO, PO Box 398166, Minneapolis, Minnesota 55439. Copyright © 2024 by Abdo Consulting Group, Inc. International copyrights reserved in all countries. No part of this book may be reproduced in any form without written permission from the publisher. Essential Library™ is a trademark and logo of Abdo Publishing.

Printed in the United States of America, North Mankato, Minnesota.
052023
092023

Cover Photo: Nixx Photography/Shutterstock Images (front and back)
Interior Photos: Arunee Rodloy/Shutterstock Images, 1; Dennis van de Water/ Shutterstock Images, 3, 30; Shutterstock Images, 4–5, 9, 11, 14, 20, 22, 31, 38, 41, 42, 44, 48, 50, 53, 54, 56, 74, 88, 91, 100, 101; M Production/Shutterstock Images, 7, 35; Karel Zahradka/Shutterstock Images, 17, 32; Artokoloro/Alamy, 21; VCG Wilson/Fine Art/Corbis Historical/Getty Images, 25; Andrey Armyagov/Shutterstock Images, 26–27; Chonlasub Woravichan/Shutterstock Images, 28; Bruno Cavignaux/Biosphoto/ SuperStock, 47; Uli Deck/picture alliance/Getty Images, 49; He/Imaginechina/ AP Images, 60; Dushko Vladimir/Shutterstock Images, 62; Sebastian Captures/ Shutterstock Images, 65; Tatiana Belova/Shutterstock Images, 66; Benny Marty/ Shutterstock Images, 67; Elizaveta Galitckaia/Shutterstock Images, 68; City of Burnsville/AP Images, 72; Christophe Archambault/AFP/Getty Images, 78; Jurgen Freund/Nature Picture Library/Alamy, 79; iStockphoto, 82–83; David Grimwade/ Alamy, 83; Toxotes Hun-Gabor Horvath/Shutterstock Images, 84; Diego Urdaneta/ AFP/Getty Images, 86; Angelika Warmuth/AFP/DPA/Getty Images, 94; Lea Suzuki/ The San Francisco Chronicle/Hearst Newspapers/Getty Images, 96; Nicolas Orallo/ Shutterstock Images, 99

Editor: Marie Pearson
Series Designer: Becky Daum

Library of Congress Control Number: 2022948875

PUBLISHER'S CATALOGING-IN-PUBLICATION DATA

Names: Edwards, Sue Bradford, author.
Title: Fish / by Sue Bradford Edwards
Description: Minneapolis, Minnesota: Abdo Publishing Company, 2024 | Series: Essential pets | Includes online resources and index.
Identifiers: ISBN 9781098290542 (lib. bdg.) | ISBN 9781098276720 (ebook)
Subjects: LCSH: Pets--Juvenile literature. | Aquarium fishes--Juvenile literature. | Fishes--Juvenile literature. | Pets--Behavior--Juvenile literature. | Zoology-- Juvenile literature.
Classification: DDC 636.0887--dc23

CONTENTS

MOVING DAY

Isabella checked her calendar and made sure that today was the day to relocate her new goldfish into their new tank. Her father had helped her select the fish a month ago, and since then they had been living in a quarantine tank. She had isolated them from her other fish to make sure they were healthy before moving them to her main aquarium. She checked them once again and observed that their color was still vibrant and both goldfish were swimming with their fins fully extended. Clamped fins could indicate that they were stressed or possibly sick, but they appeared healthy.

Isabella turned off the aquarium light but didn't immediately remove the lid, called a hood, that covered the top of the aquarium. Instead, she retrieved the bucket she used when she siphoned out water to clean the tank. The bucket had to be used only with the fish tank. If someone used it

Goldfish are among the most popular fish for aquariums.

POND FISH

Although goldfish can be kept in an aquarium, the goldfish available in pet stores are very young and will continue to grow. A healthy goldfish such as a fantail can easily reach six to eight inches (15–20 cm) in length, although some reach ten to 12 inches (25–30 cm) and require an especially large aquarium.[1] To provide their fish with sufficient space, some people keep goldfish in ponds, although not all varieties of goldfish can survive the winter outdoors in areas that get extremely cold.

to wash a car or mop a floor, detergent would leave a residue in the bucket and expose her fish to potentially deadly chemicals.

Placing the bucket beside the quarantine tank, Isabella removed the hood and gently set it aside, careful not to damage its light. Then she reached into the tank and, one by one, removed the decorative plants. The plastic plants didn't add oxygen to the water as real plants would, but they helped provide shelter so a stressed fish had somewhere to hide. Left in the aquarium, the plants could also make it harder to capture the fish. By the time the plants were in the bucket, Isabella's hand was wet, so she could safely handle the fish. If her hand were dry, handling a fish could accidentally remove the protective slime coating that covered the fish's scales.

Next Isabella dipped a net into the aquarium. Coming up behind the white-and-orange fantail goldfish, she gently scooped the fish into the net. At the surface of the water, she carefully put a hand over the net to keep the

fish from jumping out. Walking to her main aquarium, she
opened the lid and lowered the goldfish into the water.
She repeated the process with the second fish, a redcap
oranda goldfish, adding it to her primary aquarium.

As she completed the job, her brother Alexander
entered the room. He leaned over and peered into the
aquarium. "I know you think they're pretty, but why don't
you get something more interesting than goldfish?"
he asked.

Isabella shrugged while keeping her attention on the
fish. She wanted to be certain the original goldfish weren't
bullying the newcomers. One reason she liked goldfish
was that they were lively and interested in each other

When netting fish, it's important to move
the net slowly to avoid stressing the fish.

OTHER AQUARIUM PETS

but not aggressive. Still, adding two new fish changed the tank dynamic, and it was a good idea to make certain the introduction went smoothly. "What kind of fish would you get?" she questioned her brother.

"I like the marine fish the best, especially the ones with the bright colors like yellow sailfin tangs, damselfish, and clown fish. I know you can't mix saltwater fish with freshwater fish, but sharks are exciting and some of them live in fresh water. You could get one of those," said Alexander.

Isabella was relieved to see that her original goldfish were swimming around but paying more attention to her than to the new fish. Her original goldfish knew that she was the one who fed them, so even when it wasn't time to be fed, they watched her closely. "Do you want to feed them?" she asked Alexander.

"But it's not their mealtime," her brother responded.

Isabella explained, "We can give them a special treat every now and then."

Alexander pointed to the new goldfish, still behind the plants. "Will they get any of it way back there?" he asked.

Isabella had to admit that they probably wouldn't. Fancy goldfish weren't fast swimmers, and the original goldfish near the top of the aquarium would get to the food first. "Do me a favor," she said to Alexander. "Turn off the light and let's see what happens."

Alexander gently closed the hood and then clicked off the aquarium light. As Isabella and her brother watched, the original goldfish swam more slowly. The new goldfish didn't yet explore the tank, but they rose slightly, leaving their hiding place. "With the light off, all of the goldfish will calm down and relax a little bit."

"Like when Aunt Rebecca covers her parakeet's cage?" asked Alexander.

"Exactly, but seriously, what kind of fish would you get if you had your own aquarium?"

Alexander didn't answer immediately. "I really like the marine fish, but we saw a documentary about them in school. I don't want a fish that lived in the wild before getting stuck in an aquarium, and most marine fish come from the wild."

Isabella replied, "I understand. I'm not even sure that fancy goldfish would do well in an outdoor pond. Sure, they can grow to the size of Dad's hand, but they still swim slowly. There are birds that eat fish and so do raccoons. But indoors I can make sure they have what they need and they're safe. If you want an aquarium, you could get fish that come from a breeder and weren't captured in the wild."

Isabella pulled out her phone. "Let me show you some photos from the fish show. These are all fish from breeders—they weren't captured in the wild." Isabella swiped through her photos of the enormous central aquarium with pacus and other huge fish. Soon she and her brother were looking at photos of colorful small fish like guppies and tetras. He stopped her at a photograph of a velvety black fish with a large tail and flowing fins. "That's a molly. They aren't always black," said Isabella. "I thought you liked colorful fish?"

Alexander replied, "I do, but I really like this one too."

After dinner, Isabella and Alexander checked on the goldfish. The new fish were swimming around in the aquarium, but the original goldfish swam over to look at the siblings. "They know it's dinnertime," said Isabella. "If we always feed them at the same time, the new goldfish will behave like this too." Isabella clicked on the aquarium light and reached into the cabinet for the food. She held the bag out to her brother. He took it with a smile and fed the six goldfish several pinches of food.

Goldfish will often greet their owners by swimming to the front of the tank.

HOME AQUARIUMS AND PONDS

Ornamental fish keep people company all over the world, and many of the same types of fish are popular in Europe, the Americas, and Asia. Some of these fish come from saltwater coral reefs. These marine fish include relatively small fish like the domino damselfish, which is 2.5 inches (6.4 cm) long.[2] They also include much larger fish like the blotched porcupinefish, also known as the spiny balloonfish, which is 12 to 24 inches (30–61 cm) long.[3]

When threatened, the blotched porcupinefish looks menacing because it inflates its body with air and resembles a spiky, hard-to-swallow ball. Aquarists, people who keep and maintain aquariums, can even keep venomous fish such as the common lionfish. This fish is 12 inches (30 cm) long, a measurement that doesn't include the venomous spines that cover its body.[4]

SALT, FRESH, AND BRACKISH

Different types of aquariums duplicate the water in different ecosystems where fish live in the wild. These include saltwater ecosystems like oceans and seas; brackish ecosystems such as estuaries, where rivers flow into the ocean; and freshwater ecosystems including lakes and streams. Each type of ecosystem has a different salinity, or amount of salt dissolved in the water. Salinity can be measured with a tool called a hydrometer and is stated in measurements of specific gravity. Salt-free fresh water has a specific gravity of 1.000, brackish water measures 1.005 to 1.012, and salt water measures 1.025.[5]

Not every fish enthusiast chooses a marine aquarium. Some opt instead for an easier-to-maintain freshwater aquarium. There is a variety of freshwater fish, including the truly tiny dwarf rasbora at one inch (2.5 cm) long and the much larger long-nosed elephant fish, which is nine inches (23 cm) long. Among the largest freshwater aquarium fish are ornamental goldfish known as koi. These Japanese-bred fish get so large, up to 36 inches (91 cm) long, that many live in carefully maintained outdoor ponds.[6] Others live in massive aquariums.

Fish fans don't select their pets based entirely on size or appearance. They also consider the temperament or behavior of the fish. Some prefer community fish that are happiest and healthiest when living as part of a group of various fish species. Some community fish are also shoaling fish, such as the red-finned white cloud mountain minnow, which prefers to swim around the aquarium within a group of other fish of the same kind. Some community fish are even more particular, such as the silvery diamond tetra, which prefers to live in odd-numbered groups. Still other fish, such as the large red oscar, can be aggressive to their tank mates and need a very large tank to give everyone enough space. Fish may not be the perfect pet for everyone, but many people find keeping these animals a calming, worthwhile experience.

WILD FISH, PET FISH

t is difficult to define fish in terms of where they live since crabs, sponges, and bivalves such as oysters and clams are also aquatic animals. Furthermore, some fish spend time on land, including the blotched mudskipper, which lives in Africa, Southeast Asia, and Australia. Blotched mudskippers construct their burrows in mangrove flats where they emerge from the water to graze on microalgae and other tiny organisms that grow on the surface of the mud.

But there are other ways to define fish. Fish are ectothermic vertebrates. A vertebrate is an animal with a spinal column, and an ectotherm is an animal that cannot control body temperature internally, so most fish live in warm places. All fish have gills, which are the pair of organs that extract oxygen from water, allowing the fish to breathe. Most fish have thin, overlapping scales that protect their bodies, and they are covered

Mudskippers breathe through their skin when out of the water but breathe with gills underwater.

in a slime coating that they secrete to protect their skin from parasites and bacteria.

The swim bladder is a feature unique to fish. All fish have this long, gas-filled, balloon-like organ found beneath their spinal column. The swim bladder is what makes a fish buoyant, or able to float in water. To remain in position, neither rising to the surface nor sinking to the bottom, the fish's swim bladder must take up roughly 8 percent of its body by volume.[1]

Certain types of fish, including herring, have open swim bladders, which means that the bladder is open to the animal's gut. To inflate this type of bladder, the fish swims to the surface and swallows down air. Expelling air is accomplished by burping or farting. Because of the need to gulp air, these fish normally live only in shallow waters. If a fish with an open swim bladder dives too deep, the bladder collapses and the fish sinks. Two-thirds of all fish have a closed bladder, which means that the amount

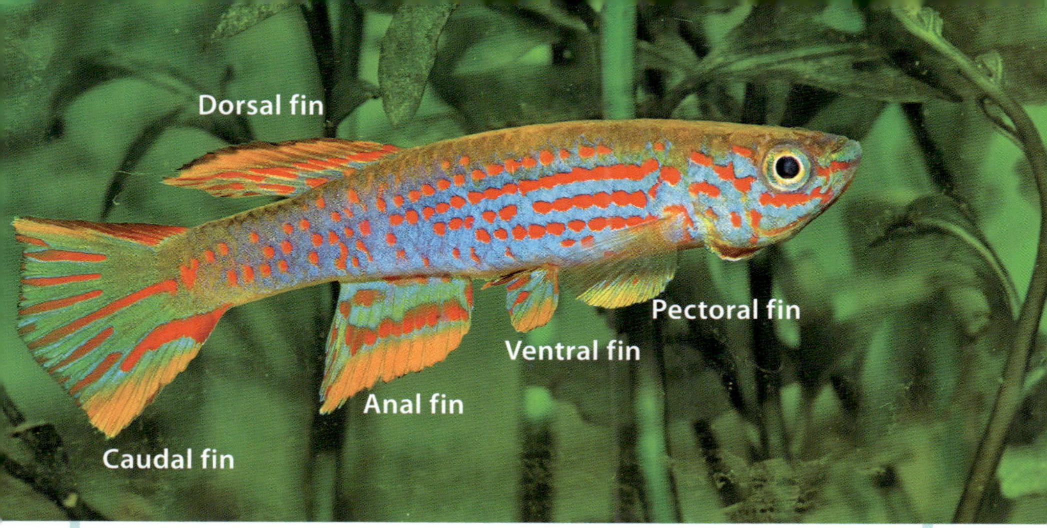

A fish's fins don't have any muscles in them. They use the muscles at the bases of the fins to make the fins move.

of gas in the bladder is altered by secreting or absorbing gas through the blood vessels. This process takes more time than swallowing air, but these fish can move more freely through multiple depths.

Fish have streamlined bodies to reduce friction so they can move quickly through water with the aid of their fins. The caudal, or tail, fin provides the thrust that drives the fish through the water. The dorsal fin that runs along the spine of most fish, as well as the anal fin located on the underside, help fish swim in a straight line. Four additional fins, two pectoral fins just behind the gills and two lower ventral fins just below the gills, help fish steer and maneuver.

How a fish looks varies depending on how it has adapted to its environment. In the wild, plecos live along river bottoms in Central and South America. They have sucker-shaped mouths that are angled downward, perfect for scraping algae off rocks and otherwise scavenging the river bottom.

Other fish are predators, adapted to pursue prey. Fish with thin *V*-shaped or crescent-shaped tails are the fastest swimmers. One of these is the barracuda, which is an ambush hunter that can briefly reach speeds of 35 miles per hour (56 kmh).[3] Barracuda and other predatory fish, such as the oceanic whitetip shark, also have sharp teeth for slicing away the flesh of prey animals. Whether they live in mangrove mudflats or the open ocean, fish have adapted both physically and behaviorally to a variety of aquatic environments. Some have features that make them better at hunting prey, while others have adapted features to escape predators.

PET FISH

When ancient peoples first started keeping fish in Sumer, Egypt, and Assyria, they were not keeping the animals as pets but as sources of food. These wild-caught fish were kept only briefly before being consumed. As early as 1000 BCE, the Chinese kept carp for food, but they raised the fish, feeding and breeding them. Gene sequencing shows that the ornamental goldfish people keep today were bred from these same carp starting more than 1,000 years ago. Chinese records show that during the Tang dynasty (618–907 CE), the most attractive carp were placed in ornamental ponds and water gardens, isolated from less attractive food fish. During the Song dynasty (960–1279 CE), the gold or yellow goldfish became the symbol of the imperial house and came to be known as the royal fish. Common people were forbidden to own goldfish of this color.

Goldfish were imported to both Japan and Europe in the early 1600s. Goldfish had a strong enough influence that on May 28, 1665, British navy administrator Samuel Pepys wrote in his diary about seeing a London friend's goldfish. These colorful fish made it to the United States around 1850 and quickly became popular.

Another early pet fish is known as the Siamese fighting fish in Europe, but they are called bettas (BEH-tuhs) in the United States. In the wild, these fish live in the canals that flow through many cities in Thailand. Recent genome sequencing shows that Thai people began breeding bettas 1,000 years ago.

GOLDFISH IN CHINA

During the Tang dynasty (618–907 CE), people selected the most attractive goldfish to keep as pets. While some were kept in garden ponds, others were placed in goldfish bowls. These were not the clear glass bowls once popular in the United States, but large ceramic pots that could be placed on decorative stands. The bowls were decorated with painted goldfish.

Today, Chinese goldfish enthusiasts recognize four modern varieties. Crucian goldfish are golden but otherwise look like wild carp. They have long, streamlined bodies and a single tail fin. When viewed from above, wen goldfish resemble the Chinese character *wen* (文). They have large heads and flared tail fins. The dragon-eye is named for its protruding eyes and has a short, thick body. The last of the varieties is known as the egg. These fish resemble eggs because they have no dorsal fins.

Goldfish remain so popular in China that every year goldfish

breeders visit the city of Zibo for a goldfish beauty
pageant. Every type of goldfish competes for the top
prize, and judges examine each fish, evaluating its size,
appearance, and expressiveness. They look for fish that
are active in the water. The 2022 winner had the habit
of swimming anytime someone stopped to investigate
its tank. When asked by reporters how much the fish
was worth, its owner refused to state a price, but
another winning fish was sold in London for $8,000.[4]

In the wild, the fish have shorter fins and duller colors and are much less aggressive than their domestic counterparts. The very first captive bettas were selectively bred for the willingness of the male fish to fight, with people pitting male fish against each other and betting large sums of money on these fights. By the end of the 1800s, the fish were popular in Europe, and breeders focused on more than aggression, selecting for appearance. This selective breeding led to a dramatic variety, with colors ranging from bright blue or red to iridescent black. Some fish were bred to have one body color and a different fin color. They were also bred for a variety of fin and tail shapes, many of which are long and draping.

> **Bettas are bred to have beautiful tails, but the tails' weight and length make them inefficient for swimming.**

THE AQUARIUM

Keeping fish in the home didn't become popular until the invention and spread of the aquarium. When Jeanne Villepreux-Power created the first aquarium in 1832, the naturalist did so to study the sea creatures that fascinated her. At the time, she called her glass invention the Power cage. *Marine vivarium* was another name for the aquarium. A vivarium is an enclosure used to raise plants and animals for scientific research. At that time, the aquarium was used only by scientists.

The London Zoo opened the first public display of aquariums in 1853. This Fish House was not built around a massive aquarium as many are today. Instead, it contained a series of smaller tanks that allowed visitors to get an up-close look at the plants and animals that live in the ocean. Scientists had only recently discovered that fish absorb oxygen from water and expel carbonic acid and that plants take in this carbonic acid and expel oxygen. This knowledge helped people create a more balanced system with both fish and plants in aquariums.

People's interest in fish grew, but the aquarium as a home accessory didn't take off until English naturalist Philip Henry Gosse published his book *The Aquarium* in 1854. At this time, there were no pet stores for people to visit to buy equipment or fish, and all aquariums were custom made based on which fish the person planned to keep. The bases of these aquariums were almost always slate, a type of stone. At least one side would be glass and the others were either glass or stone, often slate. The glass and slate slabs fitted into grooved pillars of wood that held the various pieces together. Some aquariums were rectangular while others were octagonal, and a few were glass cylinders.

Aeration, or the mixing of oxygen from the air into the water, was provided by dripping water into the tank from a device holding a seawater-soaked sponge, since only marine fish were kept. *The Aquarium* provided recipes for creating artificial seawater for anyone who lived too far from the beach to acquire the water from the ocean itself. Gosse also recommended specific plants and fish, including small sticklebacks, young gray mullet, flounder,

An illustration from 1873 advertised a traveling aquarium.

eels, and small wrasses, that these aquarium enthusiasts could capture or pay someone to catch for them.

By the end of the 1800s, England and Germany had the most aquariums, but people were also exporting fish to the United States, where the hobby was growing. Keeping warm-water tropical fish became possible only in the 1900s when the expanded availability of household electricity made it possible for people to reliably light and heat their aquariums. After World War II (1939–1945), air travel expanded globally, making it possible for breeders to ship tropical fish quickly and efficiently around the world.

CHAPTER 3

GETTING A FISH

A new aquarist has a lot to learn to be a responsible fish keeper. The needs of the fish must be met, starting with choosing fish that are compatible. This means all the fish in a single tank need to have similar water salinity needs, whether that's fresh, salt, or brackish water. Other water conditions, including the temperature and whether the water is hard or soft, also need to be similar. Water hardness is a measurement of the minerals, specifically calcium and magnesium, present in the water. Tap water is generally hard, meaning it has a high level of these minerals, and will need to be chemically softened to keep fish healthy. Water hardness affects pH, which is the measure of how acidic or alkaline the water is. Test kits make it possible to measure both the hardness and pH of tap water and aquarium water.

The tricolor shark is also called the bala shark. Despite its name, this fish is actually a minnow.

The water conditions a fish requires reflect its natural habitat. Cardinal tetras, *center*, live in calm creeks and streams in Colombia and Venezuela.

Different fish have different water requirements. For example, the tricolor shark requires a temperature of 72 to 77 degrees Fahrenheit (22–25°C), soft water with mineral levels measuring 50 parts per million (ppm), and acidic water with a pH of 6.0 to 6.5. This means the tricolor shark is not compatible with the cardinal tetra, which requires 73 to 79 degrees Fahrenheit (23–26°C), soft water measuring 0 to 50 ppm, and acidic water with a pH of 5.8.[1]

In addition to the water requirements of the fish, they must also have compatible temperaments so they will get along. Many stores label fish according to how social the animals are, with a red tag marking all fish that must live singly or else they will attack or devour tank mates. Fish with a yellow tag often have special requirements such as how much space they need or whether they need a hiding place, while fish with a green tag are good community fish.

FIRST FISH

Many different fish are good for beginners because they are hardy, thrive in a wide range of conditions, and are easy to care for. One good fish for beginners is the zebra danio, which has striking blue and silver stripes. At 1.5 inches (3.8 cm) long, zebra danios are good community fish that like to school, so they draw attention in the aquarium.[2] They also like cool water, which means that someone new to fish keeping doesn't have to closely monitor a heater.

Other small, colorful fish that are easy to keep and thrive in community tanks include neon tetras, platies, and guppies. Silver with a blue and a red stripe, the neon tetra is an attractive fish. Several must be kept together, but they are small and have little impact on water quality. This means that they don't make a lot of cleaning work for a new fish keeper. Platies and guppies have been bred to come in a variety of colors. Guppies breed easily, which can quickly overcrowd a tank if the babies find enough

SEAHORSES

Although they don't look like other fish, seahorses have gills and a swim bladder and are a variety of pipefish. There are more than 40 different species, ranging in size from less than one inch (2.5 cm) to more than 12 inches (30 cm) long.[3]

These fish are seldom found in pet stores because they are challenging to keep. Seahorses do not have stomachs, so food passes quickly through their digestive systems. This means that they need to be fed more often to get the nutrients they need to survive, usually at least four small meals a day.

Furthermore, they cannot eat fish flakes and must be fed meaty foods like brine shrimp or mysis shrimp, which are not always readily available at pet stores. Failure to provide the right food means that seahorses will not have the vitamins and minerals they need to thrive. Meaty foods can lead to poor water quality, so good filters and vigilant upkeep are a must to avoid a dirty, unhealthy aquarium. Finally, because of their tiny fins, seahorses are poor swimmers, so they often don't do well in a community tank because other fish will get to food first. Still, seahorses are attractive fish for aquarists devoted to their care.

shelter to survive. Because of this, many people keep either female or male guppies but not both.

There are also larger, colorful fish that are good for beginners who want to keep a community aquarium. Swordtails live best in groups of five or more, and each fish will reach up to 4.7 inches (12 cm) long.[4] Because of this, they need a larger aquarium than neon tetras or zebra danios. Like the swordtail, the pearl gourami eats a variety of foods. It is easier to keep than many other types of gourami. The pearl gourami needs space at the top of the tank to breathe air. It likes a place to hide, so plants are a good addition to a tank with pearl gourami.

Guppies are attractive fish that breed quickly, so they are readily available to aquarists.

The golden pheasant is a type of killifish. Males have brighter colors and longer fins than females.

Two other medium-sized fish are attractive but require space and specific conditions to live in community tanks. The betta is easy to keep because it eats a variety of foods, but two male bettas cannot be kept in the same aquarium, and a betta needs to be in a spacious aquarium. It should not be kept with fish that like to nip since its long fins are a tempting target.

Killifish are colorful, easy-to-care-for fish that require some special consideration. They are a type of cichlid, and there are many different kinds, ranging from those easily kept to more difficult ones. Red-striped killifish are good for beginners. Two females should be kept for every male so that the males don't fight over the females.

Beginning aquarists should also consider fish that help keep the tank clean, such as the tiger plecos or the cory catfish. Tiger plecos can be territorial, so it is often easier to keep just one. Cory catfish are algae eaters that do best in groups of three or more.

GEARING UP

A new fish hobbyist must make many decisions, including where to keep the aquarium. Fish are sensitive to sound. They also need a consistent temperature without drafts and need to be someplace level and strong enough to hold an aquarium full of water, such as a sturdy table. Aquariums come in many shapes and sizes. The majority are rectangular, although towers, hexagonal tanks, and corner tanks are also available. The size of the aquarium needed depends on what types of fish and how many fish it will house. Someone living in a small apartment may have space for only small fish.

NO FISHBOWLS

Pet owners shouldn't buy cheap fishbowls at thrift stores or at pet stores. These containers are tempting because they are inexpensive and don't take up much space, but fishbowls are small. There is too little water surface for a good oxygen level and no space for a heater or filter. Oxygen, the proper temperature, and clean water are all essential for healthy fish. Achieving these things requires more space than a small fishbowl provides.

Larger fish and large numbers of fish will need a bigger aquarium, and it is generally better to go as big as possible, especially if the aquarium will house goldfish. The largest goldfish reach 10 inches (25 cm) in length. Fancy goldfish do not grow as large, usually only about eight inches (20 cm) long, but goldfish are active swimmers that need space. The recommendation for fancy goldfish is to start with a 20-gallon (76 L) tank for one fish and add at least ten gallons (38 L) in size for each additional fish. This means a 55-gallon (208 L) tank could house four fancy goldfish.[5]

The list of items needed in addition to the aquarium includes substrate, a filter, and possibly a heater. The substrate is the material that covers the bottom of the tank and is usually clean gravel or sand purchased from a pet supply store. The filter keeps the water clean and, depending on the design, can be located on the side of the aquarium or under the substrate. If the filter is on the side of the tank, the water can be aerated as it is circulated, adding oxygen essential for the health of the fish. Although most goldfish do not require a heater, most other fish will need one at least some of the time to keep the water at an optimal temperature.

Most aquariums also need a hood with a light because most organisms need sunlight. Sunlight lets fish see each other to communicate, and live plants need sunlight or an

artificial light that replicates sunlight to photosynthesize. Aquarium lights should be on for no more than ten hours a day to limit the growth of algae not only on the surface of the aquarium but also on plants, which can be harmed by the algae.

Many people add decorations to their aquariums, but fish keepers should understand that plants aren't decorative. Plants provide shade and shelter for fish and food for herbivorous fish. Plants also help to chemically balance the aquarium. Plants can be difficult to grow in goldfish aquariums because goldfish sift through the substrate in search of food and often uproot plants.

When the equipment has been purchased, it is time to assemble and fill the aquarium, but untreated tap water should not be added to the aquarium. Water conditioner must be used to chemically remove the chlorine and chloramine used to treat tap water to kill microbes. Instead of using tap water, some people use water that has gone through reverse osmosis, a purification process that removes all minerals. Because fish need some minerals in the water, these must be added using baking soda, Epsom salts, and water conditioner.

There are a few more steps before fish can be put in an aquarium. Once everything has been assembled and the aquarium has been filled with water, special bacteria need to be added to cycle the water. Cycling refers to the nitrogen cycle, which breaks down the waste fish produce. As fish waste and fish food decay, the ammonia level in the water rises. Ammonia is toxic to fish, but a group of bacteria called Nitrosomonas break ammonia down into nitrites. Although nitrites are also harmful, another group of bacteria called Nitrobacter break the nitrites down into nitrates, which are not harmful in small quantities and are removed during regular water changes.

Bacteria can be added to a new tank by buying a bottle of live bacteria at an aquarium store or by adding live plants to the tank. Gravel or sand from an existing aquarium can also be added to introduce the bacteria. A water test kit will reveal what step of the cycling process an aquarium has reached, and it can take at least two weeks before fish can be added. An aquarium that has cycled has a colony of bacteria living within the substrate, on the plants, and on the other surfaces in the aquarium. Some people recommend cycling an aquarium with fish in it. This should be done only in an emergency, such as when an established tank goes off balance, because an unbalanced aquarium stresses the fish.

DIY DECOR

When adding decorations to an aquarium, fish owners need to be sure to choose things with smooth edges and no chemicals that could harm the fish. Fish with flowing fins and large eyes are often the most vulnerable to injury. Copper and other metals, painted figurines, and rocks found while hiking should be left out of the tank. Instead, owners can use plants and other items purchased at the pet store.

CHAPTER 4

CARING FOR FISH

A big part of keeping fish healthy is feeding them the right foods, and with so many commercial foods available, this means choosing the right foods for each combination of fish. Many foods are available in shakers and pouches on the shelves of aquarium stores. Fish food flakes are easy to find and suitable for a variety of fish because they float on the surface for top feeders and then sink. Flakes can also be pulverized and fed to fry, the name for newly hatched fish. Pellets are good for fish that feed at the middle or bottom of the tank, with varieties of pellets made to sink at different rates. Fish food in stick form is larger than pellets and floats, making it good for larger fish such as pacus. Fish that feed in groups benefit from tablets because the tablets are too large to be gulped down in one mouthful, so a single fish can't eat the whole thing.

Fish owners should research the needs of each species of fish they keep to decide on the right kind of food.

EATING WHERE?

It's important to know what a tank's fish eat—plant matter, meat, or a combination of the two. It is equally important to consider where in the aquarium the fish eat, because this affects which type of commercial food is best. Some fish feed at the surface and do well with sticks and flakes. Other fish feed in the middle of the tank where they can seize round pellets. Bottom-feeders will discover dissolved flakes, sunken tablets, and fish wafers that slowly absorb water and can be scraped away. It is vital that fish find their food where they naturally feed.

Tablets can also be stuck to the side of the aquarium at any level.

Meaty foods are available frozen or fresh. Two popular choices are brine shrimp, which hatch easily from eggs but also come frozen, and daphnia, tiny crustaceans that are usually a good choice for smaller fish. Bloodworms are often available, as are mosquito larvae, which are commonly fed to surface-feeding fish.

Because many fish eat plants in the wild, fresh vegetables can supplement their diets. For bottom-feeding catfish and certain cichlids, sliced cucumber or zucchini are a good source of vitamins and roughage. Bottom-feeding fish can eat frozen or shelled fresh peas, although canned peas must be avoided because of the salt they contain.

Depending on where the fish live in the wild, some eat a variety of foods, and others primarily eat one thing. One fish that eats a variety of things is the transparent glass

catfish, which feeds on flakes, freeze-dried foods, and smaller live foods. The saltwater yellow-headed jawfish, a type of goby, eats only fresh and thawed meat-based foods. Fancy goldfish eat a variety of flakes, pellets, and live foods. Depending on the species, plecos can eat either catfish food and live food or primarily vegetation.

It is vital to know what a fish eats before attempting to feed it. It is also important to make certain that shy fish and night feeders get enough to eat. One way to assure that night-feeding catfish get enough food is to drop their food into the aquarium just before turning the lights out for the night.

Many fish, including catfish, benefit from eating occasional vegetables. It's important to scrub vegetables under cool water with a stiff brush to remove pesticides before putting them in the tank.

Food packets seldom come printed with information about how much or how often to feed fish. This is because these things will depend on how many fish live in an aquarium and the size of the fish. It is best to feed small amounts often, perhaps four times a day, until it is known how much to feed. Fish should be given what they will eat in two or three minutes. Anything uneaten in five minutes should be scooped out of the aquarium with a net.[1]

Overfeeding is a problem because uneaten food will pollute the aquarium. Some fish will also overeat, which can harm their health. It can cause fatty liver disease and fin rot, shortening their life span. But underfeeding can also be a problem, since hungry fish may be aggressive with their tank mates.

KEEPING IT CLEAN

One key to keeping a healthy aquarium is a regular maintenance schedule. A new tank needs a partial water change as often as once a week, but an established aquarium may be able to go as long as one month without a water change. With any aquarium, water quality should be checked weekly.

The best time to clean is right before a water change, starting with using a scraper to remove algae from the inside of the aquarium glass. Any decorations with algae on them can also be removed and rinsed clean. Next, a siphon hose should be used to vacuum the substrate and pull decaying food and fish waste out of the aquarium. This step also helps

DAILY MAINTENANCE

The daily maintenance tasks required of an aquarist are simple. The temperature should be checked to verify whether the heater is working properly or if it needs to be adjusted. If the lights do not turn on, they should be replaced. A malfunctioning filter should be checked for blockages. This is also the time to re-anchor plants that have been uprooted by fish rooting in the substrate.

remove any clumps of algae that have come loose while scraping the inside of the aquarium. While vacuuming, approximately one-third of the water can be removed from the aquarium.

When adding water during tank maintenance, it is important to remember to use a container set aside only for aquarium maintenance to keep the fish from being exposed to harmful chemicals. The water must be prepared as it was before setting up the new aquarium,

which is why a water test kit and the necessary chemicals and additives to prepare tank water should always be available. To avoid shocking fish with cold water, after the water has been conditioned it should be allowed to come up to room temperature before being carefully and gently added to the aquarium. Regularly cleaning the aquarium is an important part of keeping healthy fish. If fish become lethargic or look unwell, their water should be tested immediately to ensure that ammonia or nitrites have not accumulated.

FISH ILLNESS

An aquarist who has carefully observed the fish in an aquarium can often tell when a fish is sick. A healthy fish is alert and swims around the tank, eating as usual, and has clear body coloration. A sick fish may stop eating or eat less, struggle to swim or swim tilted to one side, clamp its fins, and hide away from the other fish. It may rapidly pump its gills, appear to be gasping at the water's surface, or rub itself along rocks and other objects.

The symptoms displayed by a sick or injured fish are often the key to what is wrong. Identifying the ailment is the first step in treatment. Some symptoms can be seen by checking the fish's eyes. Sometimes a fish's eyes bulge from the eye sockets because of a bacterial infection. The area around the fish's eyes may also look white from a viral

AGGRESSIVE FISH

No matter how carefully fish are chosen to avoid aggression, sometimes one fish will bully its tank mates. There are ways to reduce this, starting with rearranging the aquarium and adding new hiding places to force all fish to establish new territories. A divider or small isolation tank within the main aquarium can let the bully smell other fish without attacking them and often ends aggressive behavior. If nothing else works, the aggressive fish may have to live in another aquarium alone or in a single-species group.

infection, or an eye may be missing, which most often is the result of an attack.

The fins are another indicator of health and disease. Clamped fins and lethargic behavior may indicate that the water is too cold. If white spots appear on the fins, it may be a sign of an illness known as white spot that is especially common in mollies. Fins with ragged edges and bloody streaks are indicative of fin rot, which can be the result of poor water quality and the need for better tank maintenance. It can also be caused by an attack by a tank mate.

Changes in coloration can be tricky to read because such changes may vary based on the type of fish. A stressed discus turns a solid dark color, while an oscar turns pale. Washed-out coloring in neon tetras can be caused by the parasitic infection that causes neon tetra disease. Washed-out coloring can also be the result of chlorine poisoning because water wasn't properly conditioned before being added to the tank.

White, cottony growths can appear anywhere on the fish's body and are indicative of a fungal infection.

Infections can be caused by viruses, bacteria, fungi, or parasites and are often hard to tell apart. Sometimes help can come from books on fish care or from more experienced aquarists. Medications for many ailments can be purchased at the pet store and added to the aquarium. The amount of medication needed generally depends on the water volume. For this reason, sick fish are often moved to a separate tank for treatment.

A quarantine tank, also known as a hospital tank, should be maintained at all times so it will be ready for a sick or injured fish. Keeping a fish in a quarantine tank keeps it from being harassed or stressed out by its tank mates. It is also easier to add medication to a smaller tank than to a large community tank.

RED OSCAR

The official name of this striking fish is the marble cichlid, but the aquarium community knows it as the red oscar. In the wild, this fish lives in calm, shallow rivers and river basins. In these large bodies of water, it frequently reaches 12 to 16 inches (30–40 cm) long.[2] Oscars are omnivorous and in the wild are bottom-feeders, dining on snails, shrimp, clams, and other edibles they find on the basin floor.

When living as a pet, a single fish needs a 75-gallon (284 L) aquarium, and two fish require at least 100 gallons (379 L).[3] Because they are such large fish, they also make a large amount of waste, so keeping the tank clean is important and requires a high-quality filter. Oscars will eat live feeder fish, such as goldfish, but this isn't recommended because such fish can bring in parasites or disease. Instead, oscars should be fed specialized cichlid food supplemented with bloodworms, mealworms, fruits, and vegetables.

Oscars are not good community fish since they can be aggressive to tank mates. Because an oscar will occasionally leap out of the water, it is important that it live in an aquarium with a secure latch on the hood. Oscars need mental stimulation, so aquarists should be prepared to provide toys to give the fish something to play with. Possibilities include table tennis balls or a floating log.

If an aquarist cannot figure out what is wrong with a sick fish, it's best to consult a veterinarian. The average small-animal vet knows how to treat a dog or cat but may not know how to treat fish. Even vets who treat exotic pets like chinchillas and hedgehogs are unlikely to have any experience with fish. But major cities with aquariums or university study programs that deal with fish may have a specialist on hand. People can also check the American Association of Fish Veterinarians website to see if there are any fish vets nearby. An aquarium shop or local aquarium society may also know where to find a specialized veterinarian.

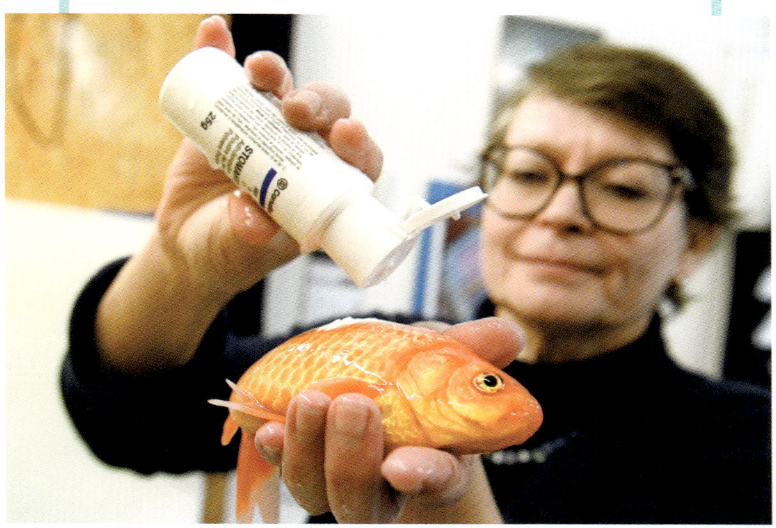

A fish veterinarian has special tools and medication for fish that regular small-animal vets do not.

CHAPTER 5

THE BUSINESS OF FISH

I n 2021, 11.8 million US households had a freshwater aquarium and another 2.9 million had a saltwater aquarium.[1] Although the United States is the world's largest importer of aquarium fish, the hobby extends around the world. To supply the demand this creates, more than 2,500 species are sold within the global fish industry. More than 60 percent of these are freshwater fish. Of the estimated 30 species that dominate the market, certain ones are consistently popular, including the neon tetra, angelfish, goldfish, zebra danio, and discus. Other popular species include fish that give birth to live young instead of laying eggs, such as the guppy, molly, and swordtail.[2]

The majority of these freshwater fish are bred in captivity for sale and exported from breeders

Angelfish are popular fish that come from the Amazon River system in South America.

in Asian countries including Singapore, which is the largest exporter; Japan; Indonesia; Sri Lanka; and Thailand. Non-Asian countries that export fish for sale include Spain, the Netherlands, the Czech Republic, Colombia, and Israel. Most saltwater fish and other saltwater aquarium animals are not bred in captivity. In 2022, it was estimated that more than 90 percent of saltwater fish in pet stores and in public aquariums had been captured and removed from the wild.[3] Whether pet fish are captured or captive bred, there are a variety of products available to help keep them healthy.

FISH FOOD AND MORE

Three of the leading companies that make fish food and aquarium products are Tetra, Sera, and Ocean Nutrition. Tetra products include specialty foods for a wide variety of tropical fish, such as tetras, bettas, plecos, and cory catfish. Other products include bacteria and conditioning

Pet stores carry many of the leading fish brands.

products to add to water before using it in the aquarium, aquarium kits, decorations, filters, and lighting.

Sera produces a similar range of products including foods, aquarium supplies, and products to treat sick fish. Unlike Tetra, Sera produces foods and aquarium supplies for both freshwater and saltwater aquariums. This includes not only water conditioners and filtering equipment but also a variety of testing supplies.

Ocean Nutrition focuses on marine fish, offering both dry and frozen foods for saltwater fish. It also sells feeding accessories including feeding stations to hold food and

Fish supplies can be purchased online, but shopping at an aquarium store can help a new fish owner get expert advice.

clips to hold seaweed. The company sells a small range of items for bettas, including foods and a water conditioner.

Whenever possible, an aquarist should shop at a local aquarium store for the best selection of quality foods and aquarium products. The staff will be able to answer questions and share information about these products. A general pet store, such as a chain store, may not have workers with expertise in fish. The staff at a store that specializes in aquariums and fish will likely have deeper knowledge about aquatic animals and their care. Someone who wants to keep an aquarium but doesn't have a nearby aquarium store or general pet store may have to go online for what they need.

THE EXPENSE

The cost of setting up and maintaining an aquarium varies greatly depending on the size of the tank and the expense of the fish. The larger the tank, the more it will cost for the substrate, decorations, other supplies, and the aquarium itself. In 2022, a typical 55-gallon (208 L) aquarium could cost almost $200.[5]

A 20-gallon (76 L) aquarium cost about $100.[6] Someone who is setting up an aquarium for the first time can save a little money if they can find a starter kit that contains the basics—a tank, hood, light, thermometer, net, heater, and filter. Buying these supplies packaged together will cost less than buying each piece individually.

The cost will also depend on whether the person is setting up a saltwater aquarium or a freshwater aquarium. A saltwater aquarium requires the same basic equipment as a freshwater aquarium plus saltwater mix and a protein skimmer to remove organic waste. It also needs live rock, which is a hard base such as a coral skeleton with many organisms living on it, such as algae and sponges. This introduces helpful bacteria to the aquarium. Because of these additions and the cost of the fish, a saltwater aquarium will cost approximately $1,000 per year to maintain. A freshwater aquarium will cost anywhere from $200 to $700 per year.[7] Much of this variability depends on what type of fish someone decides to keep. In 2022, a male betta at a large chain pet store cost as little as $7 or $8. At the same time, a larger freshwater fish such as

Saltwater aquariums may be more expensive than freshwater aquariums, but some aquarists think it's worth the expense to enjoy the wider variety of brightly colored fish.

a red oscar cost $14, while small fish like a zebra danio cost only $2.30 apiece.[8] Although a few saltwater fish are a similar price—a variety of blue damselfish cost $10 in 2022—most saltwater fish cost far more.[9] For example, an emperor angelfish was $165.[10] Stocking a saltwater aquarium can be a very expensive undertaking depending on the variety of fish.

There are multiple ways to save money. One is to buy used aquariums and other equipment from someone who has decided to quit keeping fish or has purchased a new aquarium. Another possibility is to adopt fish instead of buying them. Not everyone can take their fish with them when they move, and these people often need to rehome their fish. Notices about used aquariums and fish that need new homes may be found on the bulletin board at a local aquarium supply store.

Reducing the amount of electricity an aquarium requires is another way to save money. One way to limit the electricity required is to stock the aquarium with goldfish or other fish that don't require a heater. Another way to limit electricity is by using high-efficiency LED lighting.

FELLOW FISH HOBBYISTS

One of the most exciting things about a new hobby is sharing it with other people. New fish keepers should ask at their local fish store about organizations for fellow fish lovers. They may find a general group of tropical fish keepers or a group devoted to something specific like maintaining outdoor ponds or live reefs or keeping bettas. Some organizations will be local to one city, such as Saint Louis Area Saltwater Hobbyists, while others will be statewide, such as the Missouri Aquarium Society.

Many organizations offer benefits to members and other fish lovers. For example, with Saint Louis Area Saltwater Hobbyists, nonmembers can attend meetings and access online forums where they can discuss keeping fish with a variety of people. In this organization, only members can borrow expensive equipment and win raffle prizes.

National and international organizations are an important part of the hobby community. For example, Ornamental Fish International shares the latest information on these fish with breeders and merchants. Other organizations, including the Marine Aquarium Societies of North America, include both individuals and clubs who work to educate the public about hobby marine aquariums.

There are also magazines that target home fish keepers and help them learn about their hobby. *Aquarium Hobbyist Magazine* is free online and offers articles on setting up specialty aquariums, such as an aquarium for shrimp. *Tropical Fish Hobbyist* offers a sampling of articles online covering such topics as how to prepare a pond for winter and which cichlids can live in a community aquarium.

Breed competitions and shows are another opportunity for hobbyists to engage with the community of fish lovers. Local fish stores will know of upcoming shows in the area, from all-species shows to species-specific shows such as those that focus on guppies. A new fish hobbyist may find a general show more helpful if they are still deciding which type of fish to get, because many different types of fish will be present. Although some breeders do not attend shows, instead shipping their entered fish to the location, others attend alongside their fish and might be willing to answer questions.

In a general show, the judges examine each animal. They look for the specifics that set each species apart.

In general, they look at the size of the fish, its length, the scales and whether any are missing, color patterns, and fin shape. For example, a judge looking at a guppy will look closely at the tail and dorsal fins to see if the colors match. This judge will also look for a wide triangular tail fin. Winners receive prizes such as ribbons and trophies. The competition is not the only draw at these shows, however. At many events, experts on the various types of fish will give talks or presentations and are available to answer questions. This can be a great way for a beginning aquarist to find out about this hobby and their new fish.

Some fish shows receive entries from countries around the world.

CHAPTER 6

RULES AND REGULATIONS

Some fish experts give owners guidelines to follow. These guidelines are important for the welfare of fish. Dr. Jessie Sanders, a veterinarian with Aquatic Veterinary Services, warns new fish keepers to ignore the old rule about how many fish can live in an aquarium. This outdated guideline, still included on many websites and in many fish-keeping guides, is that for every one gallon (3.8 L) of water, an aquarium can hold one inch (2.5 cm) of fish, measuring by length. If this rule were true, it would mean that a ten-gallon (38 L) aquarium could house fish with a combined length of ten inches (25 cm), but how many fish an aquarium can hold is about more than length. For example, 12 neon tetras that are each one inch (2.5 cm) long represent roughly 12 inches (30 cm) of fish length but take up a lot less space than a single 12-inch (30 cm) koi.[1]

It can be tempting to fill an aquarium with lots of fish. But it's important for fish welfare to give each animal as much room as possible.

A better way to consider optimal aquarium size is to calculate the surface area of the water in the aquarium. The greater the surface area, the greater the amount of dissolved oxygen, which means the aquarium can house more fish. The general recommendation is 12 square inches (77 sq cm) of surface area for one inch (2.5 cm) of fish.[2] This is an important concept because an aquarium shaped like a column can hold as much water as a long, rectangular aquarium, but the long aquarium with the greater surface area will have a higher level of dissolved oxygen.

Dr. Sanders explains that potential fish owners should consider how big the adult fish will ideally get. Many people think that fish will grow only as large as the aquarium allows, but Dr. Sanders warns that this isn't true. In addition to considering the size of each adult fish, people should also consider how active the species is, how territorial it is, and its body type. Koi, which are long

and active, require at least 250 gallons (946 L) of water per fish when they reach 24 inches (61 cm) long.[3]

ACQUIRING FISH

There are laws about what fish an aquarist can legally own. Some of these laws are the result of international agreements. The 1973 US Endangered Species Act made it illegal to sell plants and animals that were in danger of becoming extinct in their natural habitats. One of the animals protected by the act is the Asian arowana, a striking aquarium fish because of its large iridescent scales and the fact that it can grow three feet (0.9 m) long.[4]

Asian arowanas, *pictured*, can be more striking in color compared with other varieties, such as the silver arowana.

The arowanas found for legal sale in the United States, the silver arowana and the black arowana, are from South America. When law enforcement confiscates an illegal arowana, the fish may be turned over to a zoo for care and display.

Each US state has its own laws about which non-endangered fish people can buy. In Washington, DC, any nonvenomous fish can legally be kept as a pet, but in Massachusetts it is illegal to keep rudd, an invasive species from Europe, and certain types of piranhas, including the red-bellied piranha. The concern is that someone might dump these fish in the wild. There the

RED-BELLIED PIRANHA

Although there are a number of species of piranhas, the red-bellied piranha makes the best pet. They are colorful and the least aggressive of the piranhas. In the wild, they are omnivorous, eating plant matter and smaller fish. In captivity, they should be fed frozen fish and meat to make for easier cleanup than if they are given live prey. Not only does live prey make for a messy meal but feeder fish, including goldfish, can introduce parasites to the tank and are not always a nutritious food choice.

Piranhas are usually kept singly because an adult red-bellied piranha needs an aquarium larger than 25 gallons (95 L). If a fish enthusiast wants more than one, they must get an aquarium large enough for three of these fish, because two fish will fight for dominance.[5] The black piranha and the ruby red piranha are similar in personality to the red-bellied piranha, but finding a breeder who has these fish available will be difficult. Any other piranha that is offered for sale should be avoided, since it is most likely a wild capture and will have an aggressive personality and be harder to maintain.

fish could reproduce and become invasive, taking over
habitat and pushing out native species. If a reputable fish
store has an animal for sale, it is legal to own it in that
state. Importation of animals is carefully regulated, and a
business that breaks the law will be penalized or forced to
close, but a fish that is legal in one state may not be legal
in another.

Instead of buying fish, some people catch wild fish
from lakes, rivers, or streams. Some do this because the
fish are free and easy to capture in the wild. Others do
it because the fish are hardy and easy to keep alive, but
there are laws that affect people who decide to capture

Keeping local fish can be easier than other types of fish because they won't require a heater.

and keep these native fish. In Connecticut, it is legal to keep the fish, but it is illegal to transport a fish for release even in the waters where it was originally captured. Aquarists who want to keep native fish should check the laws in their state before moving forward with their plan.

KEEPING FISH

Once someone has fish, there may be regulations about taking care of these pets. In the United States, federal and state laws prevent animal cruelty and the torture of animals. For example, in Missouri, abandonment or neglect that leads to the suffering or death of an animal is a misdemeanor. Someone who is guilty of this type of crime in Missouri may have to pay a fine. Also in Missouri, parents are legally responsible for making sure that their children care for animals properly. Because the focus in the United States is on preventing abuse, harm, and death, state officials or a local humane society may seize animals that are severely neglected or abused. But there are few other legal standards about how people should care for their pets.

Fish keepers who want to learn about being responsible owners can check the guidelines compiled by the Federation of British Aquatic Societies. These guidelines explain the legal responsibilities fish owners in the United Kingdom have under the nation's Animal

Welfare Act. The guidelines state that pet owners are legally responsible for learning about the basic needs of their fish. They are also required to learn how their fish should normally behave and whether they do best in a community setting or individually. The guide provides information on proper feeding, what should be part of the fish's environment, and how to care for fish in outdoor ponds. There is also information about organizations to contact to learn about a particular type of fish.

NO DUMPING

Many US states have laws that prohibit dumping aquarium fish into a pond or stream. The first reason for this is that it is cruel to the fish that are dumped. They often die slowly, unable to find food or suffering in temperatures that are too cold. Many become prey for other animals.

Dumping pet fish can also be disastrous for the environment where they are discarded. Environmentalists and

US ANIMAL WELFARE ACT

Although both the United States and the United Kingdom have an Animal Welfare Act, the two are very different. The US act concerns only dogs, cats, monkeys, guinea pigs, hamsters, rabbits, and other similar warm-blooded animals. It applies to pets and certain animals used in testing, research, and exhibitions. Because the act specifies warm-blooded animals, it offers fish, reptiles, and amphibians no legal protection.

conservation agents who work to preserve native plants and animals worry that the fish that do survive will have no natural predators and will reproduce unchecked. As the former pets increase in number, they will compete with native fish for food and other resources. Native fish may also become prey to these newcomers. When a non-native animal outcompetes local wildlife, it is considered an invasive species.

Goldfish can be a serious problem when released. In 2015, Colorado officials visited a lake in Boulder where they estimated that 3,000 to 4,000 goldfish were competing for resources with native species like channel catfish, bluegills, and sunfish.[6] In August 2022, wildlife biologists in Utah took a survey of the species living in ponds and lakes throughout the state. They found one pond that contained hundreds of goldfish.[7] Goldfish worry biologists because they can tolerate cold weather and eat a lot of food in large quantities, including snails,

Goldfish can grow very large and have been found in lakes and ponds across the United States.

insects, fish eggs, and young fish. Goldfish also stir up mud while feeding, which makes the water cloudy and reduces sunlight, making it harder for aquatic plants to grow.

Another species periodically discovered in US ponds and lakes is the pacu. Juvenile pacus are sold as pets, but some species grow up to five inches (13 cm) in length in an aquarium and ten inches (25 cm) long in the wild.[8] Owners who no longer want their pets sometimes dump the pacus. When captured, they are often reported as piranhas with humanlike teeth, because unlike the piranha's sharp teeth, pacu teeth are flat to grind tree nuts that fall into the water. Biologists and wildlife experts worry that a population of these fish could become established in the southern United States and outcompete local wildlife.

Concerns about invasive species are why piranhas are illegal in states like Louisiana that have mild winters. Officials worry that released pets could survive the winter and become invasive. To date, only single animals have been discovered, such as a lone red-bellied piranha caught in University Lakes in Baton Rouge, Louisiana, in May 2021. Anti-dumping laws are in place to try to keep it that way.

CHAPTER 7

FISH DEBATES

Not everyone believes that keeping fish in aquariums is acceptable even if the fish are well maintained and live longer than in the wild. People for the Ethical Treatment of Animals (PETA) is a well-known animal rights organization. Members of PETA speak out against public aquariums like Shedd Aquarium in Chicago, Illinois. PETA's stance is that the aquariums are exploiting the animals that live there and are "an example of human supremacy."[1] PETA believes that freshwater and saltwater fish that live in aquariums suffer because they are confined. PETA concedes that some people find watching aquariums soothing and recommends that these people watch a video instead.

Organizations like PETA promote animal rights, which can include the belief that animals should not be used by humans for any reason, no matter how well cared for they are. Some people who support animal rights also believe that life in captivity is wrong for all animals. Animal rights organizations sometimes take

Some people mistreat fish, such as by making them live in dirty water. This has led to debates about whether more laws are needed or if fish should be kept as pets at all.

part in controversial activities that others say are equally harmful to an animal's well-being. A writer for the large animal sanctuary Best Friends Animal Society, Gregory Castle, says of PETA, "They believe that most people can't be trusted with the care of a pet, but rather than keep them under lock and key [like a hoarder with the same thought], PETA simply kills them or advocates for killing them. They, too, are blind to the effects of depriving an animal of its most fundamental right—the right to life."[2]

However, members of PETA aren't the only ones who question the ethics of the ornamental fish trade. The Animal Welfare Institute challenges the lack of regulation in the ornamental fish industry as well as the public's lack of knowledge about how wild capture impacts both wild populations and the captured animals. This group says

GASPING FOR BREATH?

Sometimes a fish appears to be gasping at the water's surface. Bettas and gouramis are anabantoids, a group of fish that can occasionally breathe air at the surface. Near the gills, these fish have a labyrinth organ that pulls oxygen from the air. They seldom use this organ, so spending a lot of time at the surface may indicate oxygen in the water is low. Another sign of this is fish remaining in the upper portion of the tank where oxygen levels are naturally higher. The easiest way to increase oxygen levels is to move the filter to disrupt the surface of the water or to add an air bubbler.

that 80 percent of the fish captured in the wild for sale into the pet trade die because of stress, injury, disease, or mistreatment.[3]

Animal welfare groups have a different approach than do animal rights groups. The goal of welfare organizations is to ensure that animals are well cared for, acknowledging that, for a variety of reasons, animals bred in captivity are unfit for life in the wild. Animal welfare groups work to ensure that pets and other captive animals have healthy lives. These groups don't object to goldfish living in aquariums. However, they do object to the crowded aquariums and poor water conditions found in some pet stores. Stores with crowded tanks may care more about creating dramatic displays full of fish to entice people to buy them than they do about healthy aquariums. Animal welfare supporters educate others about how to properly care for animals.

These same organizations also challenge the practice of using living fish as prizes at carnivals, where they are handed out in small bowls or even cups. They are against this practice in part because the families who receive these prizes don't have the opportunity to consider the commitment they are making. They may not know how to properly care for the fish. Yet another practice these groups challenge is dyeing fish, as happens with stained glass fish. A person usually uses a needle to inject dye into

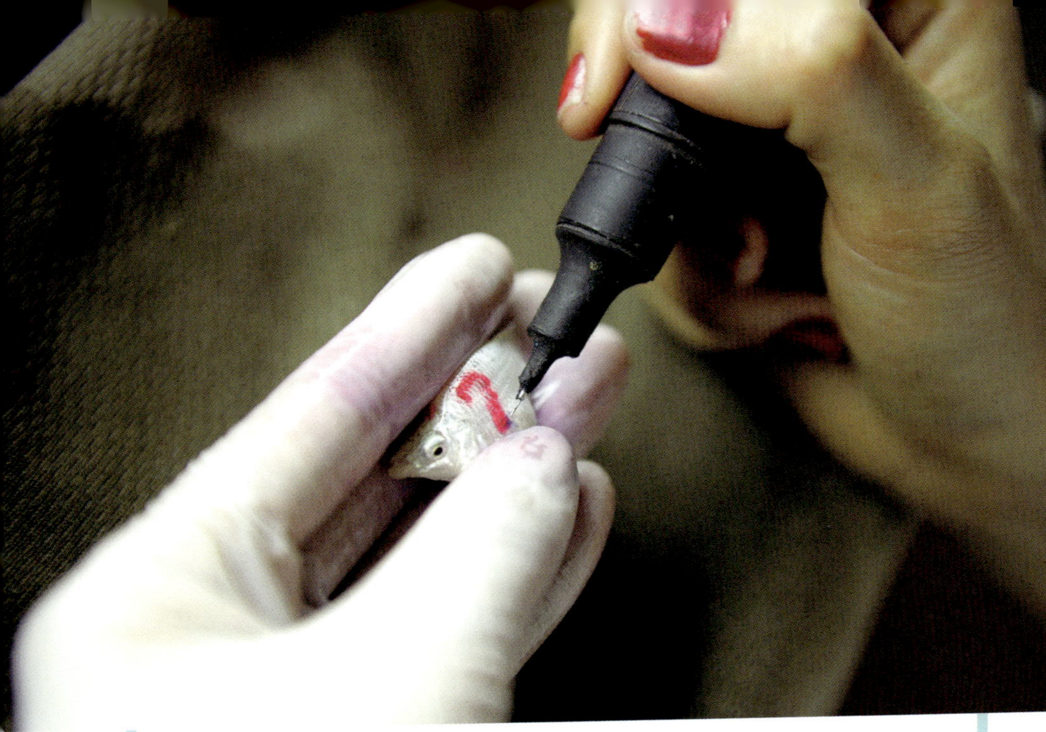

When dyeing fish, disease can spread through a shared needle.

the fish. It may be painful to the fish, and it causes a high rate of disease and death.

AGAINST WILD CAPTURES

Perhaps one of the most controversial practices in the fish trade is the capture of wild fish for sale. In 2021, 2.9 million US households kept marine fish.[4] In 2020, it was estimated that 50 million coral reef animals, including fish, corals, and other invertebrates, were removed from the ocean each year to be sold and to stock saltwater aquariums.[5] The problem isn't just how many creatures are removed from the wild but also how they are removed.

One controversial capture method involves the use of poisonous cyanide tablets crushed up in plastic squirt bottles. Seawater is mixed with the crushed cyanide and squirted into the coral, where the poisonous substance kills coral and up to 50 percent of the exposed fish.[6] Other fish are stunned and then captured.

This practice is fatal to more sea creatures than those that die immediately. Additional fish die within hours of exposure to the poison. Still others die during the next week. The Humane Society International explains that

Cyanide poisoning happens in reefs around the world, including in the Philippines.

cyanide isn't the only thing that kills fish captured in the wild. Others die from being brought to the surface after being captured at a great depth. This change from being deep in the ocean to being on the surface causes barotrauma, which in human divers is known as decompression sickness. Visible symptoms of barotrauma in a fish include bulging eyes and a bulging cloaca, the cavity from which waste is expelled.

These fish are brought to the surface too quickly for their swim bladders to adjust, so they are subjected to a process called fizzing. The person catching the fish uses a needle to stab through the fish's flesh to its swim bladder. This damages the fish's skin, scales, muscles, and the swim bladder itself. It is estimated by For the Fishes, an organization that protects coral reef habitats, that for every marine fish that is sold, six more die.[7]

PROVIDING JOBS

Although they do not support capture methods that abuse fish, some conservationists back the trade of wild-captured tropical fish. They point out that the capture and sale provide jobs and a good income for local people. Legal sales of fish and other marine life that are exported abroad can be taxed, providing income for local governments. Because of this, sustainable wild-capture programs give governments an incentive to protect the reefs and rain forests where these animals live.

Even with this support, changes are being made in how marine wildlife is brought into the market. Net capture is increasingly common, as is the push to breed a greater variety of marine fish in their local environments. Till Deuss is the founder of Bocas Mariculture, a company he operates out of Panama. When Deuss first visited Panama, he was impressed by the marine environment but also saw signs of overfishing. Local communities were having trouble supporting themselves by taking fish from their waters.

In 2019, Deuss received the permits that he needed from the Panamanian government to export exotic fish. These fish are not wild captures but come from the Bocas Mariculture hatchery. Deuss employs local people in aquaculture to grow corals. Bocas Mariculture currently provides sustainably grown coral, sea urchins, shrimp, and a small selection of fish to the aquarium market.

FISH IN THE UNITED KINGDOM

In the United Kingdom, some pet fish live in indoor aquariums and other pet fish live outdoors in garden ponds. The size of the pond depends, in part, on the size of the garden, but to have a self-sustaining pond that is easy to care for, it needs to cover at least 54 square feet (5 sq m) and be two feet (0.6 m) deep in the center.[8] Goldfish and koi are both popular choices in large ponds, as are sturgeons, which in the wild can reach 6.6 feet (2 m) long but tend to reach only 3.3 feet (1 m) long in a pond.[9] Fish give off hormones and pheromones that build up in the pond, inhibiting growth.

Wild fish that are popular pond fish include the tench and the stickleback. The tench is a bottom dweller that cleans up food overlooked by other fish and can reach 1.9 feet (0.6 m) in length.[10] The stickleback is an efficient feeder that quickly devours insects and amphibian eggs, but it is a small fish, typically reaching a size of only two inches (5 cm) long, so it cannot be kept with larger fish that might eat it.[11]

KOI

Sometimes owners need to put mesh over their fish ponds to protect them from birds such as herons.

A garden pond needs plants that float on the surface to provide shelter and plants that leaf out underwater to provide oxygen. Setting up a pond is much like setting up an aquarium in that attention must be given to pond size, maximum fish size, community needs, and water quality.

Some species of fish need a breeding tank with special conditions to cause them to breed.

Deuss sees the company's efforts as essential to the market because consumers are becoming more environmentally conscious and vocal in their demands to preserve marine environments.

Despite the work of Bocas Mariculture and other groups, relatively few marine animals are bred in captivity. In addition to finding animals that can breed in captivity, Deuss and others doing this work must breed the plankton, algae, and other microscopic sources of food that newly hatched fry rely on for their nutrition.

Deuss explains that there is little research into how to do this for the pet market, since aquaculture research has largely focused on growing human food.

UNTAMED COMPETITION

Sometimes conflicts related to the pet fish trade involve criminal activity. In 2004, a Taiping, Malaysia, shop owner was murdered and every Asian arowana he had in stock stolen. One breeder in West Java, Indonesia, reported that in 2019 approximately 400 arowanas valued at around 24 billion Indonesian rupiah, worth approximately $1.6 million in US dollars, had been stolen from his ponds.[12] Although other species of arowana are legal in the United States, Anthony Nguyen, the owner of Ichiban Tropical Fish Store in Pittsburgh, Pennsylvania, pleaded

OPERATION JUNGLE BOOK

In 2017, 16 people were prosecuted in US courts for allegedly participating in wildlife smuggling. This was part of a US Fish and Wildlife Service (USFWS) initiative called Operation Jungle Book. One of the people who pleaded guilty was Kevin Duc Vu, who sold Asian arowanas as well as several protected turtle species. US Customs and Border Patrol had discovered an illegal shipment of his in 2016. Shortly after, USFWS agents found frozen arowanas in Vu's freezer. In 2017, Vu pleaded guilty to a felony charge for illegally importing these animals. The maximum sentence for this charge is 20 years in prison.[13]

EB6
EB7
U.S.
FISH & WILDLIFE
SERVICE
DEPARTMENT OF THE INTERIOR
BOX NO
LIVE TROPICAL FISH
BOX NO
BOX NO :
LIVE TR
READE
TED BRA
THE
staples special
H2

guilty in 2021 to illegally selling both Asian arowanas and snakehead fish, which are also illegal.

As Nguyen's case shows, arowanas aren't the only fish that become the focus of criminal activity. In 2018, three people were arrested after they stole a horn shark from an open pool at a San Antonio, Texas, aquarium. They placed the small shark in a bucket and wheeled it out of the facility in a stroller. Within two days, members of the public had helped the police track down the suspects, and the shark was returned to the aquarium.

The demand for rare fish leads some people to break the law. In April 2021, the US Fish and Wildlife Service (USFWS) and Brazilian police found more than 200 aquariums of killifish and hundreds of eggs inside a home in Maryland. These fish were seized as part of a global ring of 80 people from 24 countries who were involved in illegally capturing endangered species of killifish from parklands and protected areas in the Americas, Africa, and Europe. They then used various social media platforms to arrange the sale of the fish.[14]

USFWS officials work to stop the smuggling of fish into the country.

CHAPTER 8

WONDERFUL FISH

Fish make good pets, but the perfect fish for each person is going to depend on that person and what is going on in their life. A pet that works well for a young person living at home may not be the perfect pet for a college student in a dorm room. There are a lot of fish from which to choose, and fish fans may select different fish at different times.

Goldfish owner Nancy said that she and her husband had cichlids and guppies before they had children. After they moved and spent some time without fish, they wanted something new. "I really, really love the personality and temperament . . . of goldfish. Particularly I liked the fantails," says Nancy.[1]

Pets provide people with companionship, and fish provide a particular type of enrichment. A study released in July 2015 by British researchers showed the benefits of watching aquarium fish. At the time of the

Fish can bring joy to their owners.

study, a main exhibit at the United Kingdom's National Marine Aquarium was being refurbished and fish were slowly being reintroduced. The study found that people who watched the fish in this exhibit experienced a slowing of their heart rate, decrease in blood pressure, and general improvement in their mood. As more fish were returned to the exhibit and the display became more varied and complex, people's moods further improved. The greater number of fish kept people's attention longer.

While other pets can also be a mental and physical benefit to their owners, fish have some benefits that dogs and cats do not. An apartment that does not allow a person to keep a large pet may allow them to keep fish. Fish do not relieve themselves in the yard, which eliminates the chore of having to clean up the yard. Fish do not become stressed if their owner must go to school or work for the day. Fish do not require daily walks. Fish also don't produce allergens like dander and fur the way dogs or cats do. Additionally, the latest technology has made keeping fish easier than ever before.

BETTER FISH CARE

Not only have scientists been studying how fish help people but they have also been helping people discover how to better care for their fish. This includes a better understanding of how to balance the bacteria that are

Rental properties often do not allow traditional pets such as dogs or cats because of the damage they can do. These properties may allow fish because fish won't damage the home.

essential to a healthy tank. Bacteria have changed how filtration works.

The most common form of filtration is still mechanical filtration, which uses a physical filter to capture fish waste, food, and plant material much the way a net would. The problem with mechanical filters is that accumulating particles slowly clog the filter. When water leaves the filter, it falls back into the aquarium, much like a miniature waterfall, aerating the aquarium. But as a mechanical filter becomes clogged, less water passes through it, and less aeration takes place.

New filtering technology uses bacteria that function much like the bacteria in a natural pond or stream. The first step is starting a colony of bacteria inside the filter. Water is then pulled out of the aquarium and through the filter, where the bacteria break down the various impurities. Some filters that use bacteria are shaped like canisters, but these filters are expensive. Less expensive are bio-wheel filters. These filters pull in water from the aquarium, and as the water flows back out, it flows over and through the bio wheel, which looks like a water-driven mill wheel. The wheel itself is host to bacteria, and the turning of the bio wheel aerates the water, which helps the bacteria work even more effectively. A biological filter boosts the production of nitrates and helps maintain a stable nitrogen cycle in the aquarium.

Technological advances have also led to updated lighting, with a new variety of bulbs that better mimic the qualities of sunlight. For nocturnal species, LED lighting can imitate moonlight. In addition, the LED lights use less electricity and put out less heat than older lighting technology, making it easier to control the temperature of the aquarium.

The foods that people feed their aquarium fish have also improved. Fish foods are now more nutritious and higher quality. This is especially important for marine fish, which are notoriously picky eaters. These dietary improvements combined with liquid vitamins and water conditioners have greatly improved the health of aquarium fish. Owners can pour liquid vitamins into the tank or soak food in them.

New technologies have made much of the equipment needed to maintain a healthy aquarium smaller than ever before. This has made keeping smaller tanks easier, which explains the trend toward nano tanks, small tank ecosystems complete with plants. "There are tons of nano aquariums out there today that are perfect for bettas. A lot of these nano tanks have built-in filtration and built-in lighting that makes them very easy to maintain," said John Hudson of KGTropicals.[2]

Some nano tanks come boxed and ready to go, but some prepackaged setups include tanks that are too small for almost any fish, such as ones that are just two gallons (7.6 L). Jen Clifford, a biologist and aquarist, explains that when she discusses setting up a nano tank, she means any tank from five to 30 gallons (19–114 L).[3] This is much

> Because nano tanks are small, a slight miscalculation in water conditioner or another water additive has a bigger impact on water quality than being off by the same amount in a larger tank.

bigger than many people think when they hear the term *nano tank*, but even when going small, a responsible aquarist makes certain that fish have enough space to live well.

Regardless of the tank size, aquarists can take advantage of new monitoring and timing devices. Aquarium monitors check not only the pH but also the temperature and ammonia level. Sometimes the data can be checked remotely from a smartphone. Reef aquariums and other setups that have problems with evaporation can be fitted with an automatic top-off (ATO) system that will pump additional water into the tank or out of the tank if it is about to overflow.

AQUAPONICS

New trends don't just help people keep healthier fish. They are also helping people discover that keeping fish and growing food can go hand in hand. As fish eliminate waste, their water becomes

NANO FISH

Because nano aquariums are small, the best fish for nano aquariums are also small. Still, aquarists need to be careful not to buy too small an aquarium. This is because many small fish are community fish that do best when living in groups, such as the neon tetra, the cardinal tetra, and the rasbora. A good bottom-feeder for a community nano aquarium is the salt and pepper catfish. For a nano aquarium set up around a single fish, some options are the betta or the colorful Rachow's nothobranch, a type of killifish.

nitrogen rich. Nitrogen is an important element in fertilizing plants, and fish water can be used to fertilize various food plants including vegetables. This approach to agriculture is called aquaponics.

When a fish's water is changed to keep the fish healthy, waste-filled water is often dumped into streams or natural waterways. Because of the amount of ammonia in the water, it can pollute the waterways. In aquaponics, the water that is removed from a tank is instead used to water plants. Fertilizing plants with this water also eliminates the need to use chemical fertilizers, which are often part of agriculture. The plants that fish tank water fertilizes can feed people or the fish.

Possible aquaponics setups vary based on how much space is available and what the person wants to grow. With enough space for two ponds, one can be used for fish and the other can be used to grow plants. Rafts holding plants are floated on the plant pond, with the roots dangling directly into the water. Water from the fish pond is used to fertilize the plant pond. This technique, called deep water culture, is a good way to grow salad greens.

Some people purchase aquaponics systems that go with their aquariums.

The nutrient film technique also dangles the plants' roots directly into the water. In this method, water passes through a plastic pipe with small holes in the top, and each hole holds a plant. This method is good for small plants that don't require a lot of fertilizer, like strawberries and herbs.

In another setup called media-based aquaponics, pieces of shale or clay pellets take the place of soil and can be used to grow fruiting plants, herbs, and greens. Filtered water from the fish tank is then used to water the containers of plants. Modern science helps people combine their hobbies, keeping both fish and plants.

People have kept fish for thousands of years, although how and why people keep them have evolved over time. Whether someone is an experienced aquarist or entirely new to the hobby, there are many interesting and beautiful fish they can keep. This hobby

AQUAPONICS TANK KITS

Aquarists who want to try their hand at aquaponics can buy kits to go with their aquariums. These kits include a garden bed supported on legs so that it will stand over the aquarium, a planting medium such as soil or clay pellets, a pump to move water from the aquarium to the planting tray, and a grow light for the plants. This type of setup is small enough to fit on a counter, and the plants can be easily moved so owners can access the aquarium and care for the fish inside.

continues to change as advancing scientific knowledge and improvements in technology help people take better care of their fish.

OWNING A FISH

Fish are beautiful and relaxing, but they require very specific conditions to thrive in captivity. Many new fish keepers, or aquarists, decide to keep freshwater fish because they are easier to keep than saltwater fish.

DIET: Fish should be fed only what they will eat in two to three minutes.

SPACE: Types of fish must be carefully chosen so that they are compatible with each other and have the same water needs. Not all fish live well in groups. Once the type of fish has been chosen, a suitably large aquarium should be purchased.

ROUTINE CARE: Once fish have been added to the aquarium, a schedule must be set up for water changes and other maintenance.

ENRICHMENT: To keep fish from becoming bored, owners should rotate and move tank decorations. Fish can also be taught tricks.

KEY SPECIES

- Bettas are colorful fish that are fairly easy to keep, but two male bettas cannot live in the same aquarium.
- Goldfish are easy to keep but require space to grow.
- Guppies are colorful fish that are smaller than bettas and make good members of community tanks. They breed easily, so many people keep one sex or the other.
- Killifish are a group of several species. They are colorful, small cichlids. Killifish are somewhat aggressive, and some kinds can be kept only with other killifish.
- Neon tetras are small community fish that do best when kept in groups.
- Red oscars are large, attractive cichlids that are often kept individually because of the space required to keep them.
- Seahorses are a group of several species. They are saltwater fish that are attractive but difficult to keep because they must be frequently fed.
- Zebra danios are attractive, striped fish that make good members of community tanks.

GLOSSARY

adapted
Possessing inherited traits that allow an individual or species to be more successful in its environment.

ambush hunter
A sit-and-wait predator that uses surprise and a quick chase to capture its prey.

aquaculture
The process of raising fish and other aquatic animals for food.

aquaponics
Using wastewater from fish to water and fertilize food plants.

bivalve
A shellfish with a hinged shell, such as a clam or oyster.

brackish
Slightly salty, such as the conditions in the water where river water and seawater mix in estuaries.

colony
A growing cluster of bacteria.

genome sequencing
Finding the order of the full genetic material of a species.

hatchery
A place where fish eggs are hatched under human care.

invasive species

An organism that arrives in a new ecosystem, takes over, and causes harm.

parts per million (ppm)

A calculation to describe the amount of something found in water based on how many parts of that thing are in a sample of one million parts of that water.

polyp

The solitary form of coral. Each polyp has a cylindrical body and a mouth surrounded by tentacles.

reverse osmosis

A process in which water is passed through a membrane to remove minerals.

roughage

Food that is largely indigestible and rich in fiber to help stool pass through the body.

secrete

To form and release a substance.

siphon

A tube used to draw water out of an aquarium.

specific gravity

The ratio of one substance's density compared with the density of another substance, based on the weight of each in air.

SELECTED BIBLIOGRAPHY

Alderton, David. *Encyclopedia of Aquarium and Pond Fish.* DK, 2019.

Bester, Cathleen. "*Sphyraena Barracuda*: Great Barracuda." *Florida Museum*, n.d., floridamuseum.ufl.edu. Accessed 17 Oct. 2022.

"Cichlid: *Cichlidae.*" *San Diego Zoo*, n.d., animals.sandiegozoo.org. Accessed 17 Oct. 2022.

Jennings, Greg. *500 Freshwater Aquarium Fish*. Firefly, 2018.

"Your Legal Duty of Care for Keeping Fish under the Animal Welfare Act." *Federation of British Aquatic Societies*, 2008, fbas.co.uk. Accessed 17 Oct. 2022.

FURTHER READINGS

Alderton, David. *The Complete Practical Guide to Small Pets & Pet Care*. Lorenz, 2021.

Krekelberg, Alyssa. *Essential Fish*. Abdo, 2022.

Perdew, Laura. *Animal Conservationists*. Abdo, 2020.

ONLINE RESOURCES

To learn more about pet fish, please visit **abdobooklinks.com** or scan this QR code. These links are routinely monitored and updated to provide the most current information available.

MORE INFORMATION

For more information on this subject, contact or visit the following organizations:

International Coral Reef Society (ICRS)

89111 Overseas Hwy.
Tavernier, FL 33070
coralreefs.org

The ICRS is a group of researchers, scientists, teachers, and students from more than 70 countries working to educate the public and preserve coral reefs for the future.

Museum of Natural History, University of Colorado Boulder

15th and Broadway
Boulder, CO 80309
cumuseum@colorado.edu
colorado.edu/cumuseum/life-colorados-freshwater

The exhibit "Life in Freshwater" details freshwater life in Colorado. It is both online and at the museum.

Shedd Aquarium

1200 S. DuSable Lake Shore Dr.
Chicago, IL 60605
contactus@sheddaquarium.org
sheddaquarium.org

In addition to the various aquatic exhibits and animals for visitors to view, the Shedd Aquarium is a leader in conservation. These efforts include habitat cleanups and reducing the amount of plastic being discarded, which often pollutes waterways.

SOURCE NOTES

CHAPTER 1. MOVING DAY

1. Alison Page. "Fantail Goldfish: The Right Way to Care for Fantails." *Goldfish Tank*, 26 Apr. 2022, thegoldfishtank.com. Accessed 31 Jan. 2023.

2. David Alderton. *Encyclopedia of Aquarium and Pond Fish*. DK, 2019. 240.

3. Jessica Kenzie. "*Diodon Holocanthus*: Blotched Porcupine." *Animal Diversity Web*, n.d., animaldiversity.org. Accessed 31 Jan. 2023.

4. Alderton, *Encyclopedia of Aquarium and Pond Fish*, 265.

5. "Brackish Fish." *Aqueon*, n.d., aqueon.com. Accessed 31 Jan. 2023.

6. Alderton, *Encyclopedia of Aquarium and Pond Fish*, 78, 186, 355.

CHAPTER 2. WILD FISH, PET FISH

1. David Alderton. *Encyclopedia of Aquarium and Pond Fish*. DK, 2019. 18.

2. Alderton, *Encyclopedia of Aquarium and Pond Fish*, 14–15.

3. Cathleen Bester. "*Sphyraena Barracuda*." *Florida Museum*, n.d., floridamuseum.ufl.edu. Accessed 31 Jan. 2023.

4. Jessica Novia. "The Wonderful and Wacky World of Goldfish Beauty Pageants." *Goldthread*, 20 Nov. 2020, goldthread2.com. Accessed 31 Jan. 2023.

CHAPTER 3. GETTING A FISH

1. David Alderton. *Encyclopedia of Aquarium and Pond Fish*. DK, 2019. 74, 99, 140.

2. Stanley H. Weitzman. "Teleost." *Encyclopedia Britannica*, 15 Nov. 2018, britannica.com. Accessed 31 Jan. 2023.

3. Katie Hogge. "7 Wild Facts You May Not Know about Seahorses." *Ocean Conservancy*, 10 Dec. 2018, oceanconservancy.org. Accessed 31 Jan. 2023.

4. "13 Best Freshwater Fish for Beginners." *Fishkeeping Advice*, n.d., fishkeepingadvice.com. Accessed 31 Jan. 2023.

5. Adam Jones. "Do Goldfish Need a Big Tank? Why Goldfish Tank Size Matters." *Goldfish Tank*, 26 Aug. 2022, thegoldfishtank.com. Accessed 31 Jan. 2023.

6. "Step by Step Reef Aquarium." *LiveAquaria*, n.d., liveaquaria.com. Accessed 31 Jan. 2023.

CHAPTER 4. CARING FOR FISH

1. "How to Properly Feed Your Fish." *Aqueon*, n.d., aqueon.com. Accessed 31 Jan. 2023.

2. Meredith Dowdy. "*Astronotus Ocellatus*: Marble Cichlid." *Animal Diversity Web*, 2018, animaldiversity.org. Accessed 31 Jan. 2023.

3. Saleema Lookman. "How to Care for Oscar Fish: Everything You Need to Know." *Pets Love to Know*, 29 Sept. 2021, lovetoknowpets.com. Accessed 31 Jan. 2023.

CHAPTER 5. THE BUSINESS OF FISH

1. "Pet Industry Market Size, Trends & Ownership Statistics." *American Pet Products Association*, n.d., americanpetproducts.org. Accessed 31 Jan. 2023.

2. V. K. Dey. "The Global Trade in Ornamental Fish." *INFOFISH International*, Apr. 2016, bassleer.com. Accessed 31 Jan. 2023.

3. Rob Fletcher. "Should Aquaculture Replace the Wild-Caught Pet Fish Trade?" *Fish Site*, 27 May 2022, thefishsite.com. Accessed 31 Jan. 2023.

4. "Live Ornamental Fish: Imports and Exports 2021." *Trend Economy*, n.d., trendeconomy.com. Accessed 31 Jan. 2023.

5. "Top Fin® Essentials Aquarium Starter Kit." *PetSmart*, n.d., petsmart.com. Accessed 31 Jan. 2023.

6. "Top Fin® LED Bubble Wall Aquarium Kit." *PetSmart*, n.d., petsmart.com. Accessed 31 Jan. 2023.

7. "Saltwater Filtration: How Protein Skimmers Enhance Aquarium Filtration." *LiveAquaria*, n.d., liveaquaria.com. Accessed 31 Jan. 2023.

8. "Live Fish." *PetSmart*, n.d., petsmart.com. Accessed 31 Jan. 2023.

9. "Blue Devil Damsel (*Chrysiptera Cyanea*)." *Petco*, n.d., petco.com. Accessed 31 Jan. 2023.

10. "Emperor Angelfish, Juvenile (*Pomacanthus Imperator*)—Small." *Petco*, n.d., petco.com. Accessed 31 Jan. 2023.

CHAPTER 6. RULES AND REGULATIONS

1. Jessie Sanders. "How Many Fish per Gallon?" *Aquatic Veterinary Services*, 31 May 2018, cafishvet.com. Accessed 31 Jan. 2023.

2. David Alderton. *Encyclopedia of Aquarium and Pond Fish*. DK, 2019. 30.

3. Sanders, "How Many Fish per Gallon?"

4. Emily Voigt. "A Fish So Coveted People Have Smuggled, Kidnapped, and Killed for It." *Longreads*, 18 July 2016, longreads.com. Accessed 31 Jan. 2023.

5. "Pet Piranha 101—Do Piranhas Make Good Pets?" *Geo Zoo*, 6 Nov. 2018, geozoo.org. Accessed 31 Jan. 2023.

6. Avianne Tan. "How These 3,000-Plus Invasive Goldfish Are Threatening a Whole Colorado Lake Ecosystem." *ABC News*, 7 Apr. 2015, abcnews.go.com. Accessed 31 Jan. 2023.

7. Carter Williams. "Hundreds of Goldfish Found Illegally Dumped in Utah Pond. Here's Why That's a Problem." *KSL.com*, 11 Sept. 2022, ksl.com. Accessed 31 Jan. 2023.

8. Greg Jennings. *500 Freshwater Aquarium Fish: A Visual Reference to the Most Popular Species*. Firefly, 2018. 280.

CHAPTER 7. FISH DEBATES

1. "'The Dark Hobby' Sheds Light on What the 'Pet' Fish Trade Is Doing to Hawaii's Ocean." *PETA*, n.d., peta.org. Accessed 31 Jan. 2023.

2. Gregory Castle. "PETA's 'Better off Dead' Philosophy." *Best Friends Animal Society*, 25 Jan. 2011, bestfriends.org. Accessed 31 Jan. 2023.

3. "Ethical and Ecological Implications of Keeping Fish in Captivity." *Animal Welfare Institute*, 2015, awionline.org. Accessed 31 Jan. 2023.

4. "Pet Industry Market Size, Trends & Ownership Statistics." *American Pet Products Association*, n.d., americanpetproducts.org. Accessed 31 Jan. 2023.

5. Jonah van Beijnen and Gregg Yan. "Culturing Marine Ornamentals: A $5 Billion Opportunity." *Fish Site*, 7 Dec. 2020, thefishsite.com. Accessed 31 Jan. 2023.

6. Elizabeth Claire Alberts. "People Are Killing Millions of Fish Each Year Just to Stock Aquariums." *Dodo*, 14 Apr. 2017, thedodo.com. Accessed 31 Jan. 2023.

7. Alberts, "People Are Killing Millions of Fish."

8. "How to Make a Garden Pond." *Crocus*, n.d., crocus.co.uk. Accessed 31 Jan. 2023.

9. "Pond Fish." *Maidenhead Aquatics*, n.d., fishkeeper.co.uk. Accessed 31 Jan. 2023.

10. "Tench: *Tinca Tinca*." *Maidenhead Aquatics*, n.d., fishkeeper.co.uk. Accessed 31 Jan. 2023.

11. "Stickleback: *Gasterosteus Aculeatus*." *Maidenhead Aquatics*, n.d., fishkeeper.co.uk. Accessed 31 Jan. 2023.

12. "The Theft Case of 400 Super Red Arowana Fish Worth Rp24 Billion Belonging to Irfan Hakim's Friend Was Revealed by the Police." *VOI*, 27 July 2021, voi.id. Accessed 31 Jan. 2023.

13. "Operation Jungle Book Targets Wildlife Trafficking, Leading to Federal Criminal Cases and Recovery of Numerous Animal Species." *US Department of Justice*, 20 Oct. 2017, justice.gov. Accessed 31 Jan. 2023.

14. Katie Jones. "Brazil's Cheaper Exotic Fish Still Targeted by Traffickers." *InSight Crime*, 29 Apr. 2021, insightcrime.org. Accessed 31 Jan. 2023.

CHAPTER 8. WONDERFUL FISH

1. "For Love of Fantails | Why I Chose Them." *YouTube*, uploaded by K & N Fish Room, 8 Mar. 2020, youtube.com. Accessed 31 Jan. 2023.

2. "Don't Buy a Betta Fish without Watching This First. 10 Things You Should Know about Betta Fish." *YouTube*, uploaded by KGTropicals, 3 Feb. 2019, youtube.com. Accessed 31 Jan. 2023.

3. Jen Clifford. "21 Freshwater Nano Fish—Different Types and Species Care Guide." *Tankarium*, 30 Jan. 2023, tankarium.com. Accessed 31 Jan. 2023.

INDEX

Sue Bradford Edwards is a Missouri nonfiction author who writes about culture, history, and science. She currently shares her work space with one cat, but she has previously lived with a variety of fancy goldfish, guppies, tetras, hermit crabs, and a piranha. She is the author of 25 other titles from Abdo Publishing, including *The Evolution of Reptiles* and *The Evolution of Mammals*.